DISCOVER THE MOST AMAZING...

MEGA BOOK OF
AIRCRAFT

INTERNET LINKED

CHRYSALIS CHILDREN'S BOOKS

INTERNET SAFETY

Always follow these guidelines for a fun and safe journey through cyberspace:

1. Ask your parents for permission before you go online.

2. Spend time with your parents online and show them your favourite sites.

3. Post your family's e-mail address, even if you have your own (only give your personal address to someone you trust).

4. Do not reply to e-mails if you feel they are strange or upsetting.

5. Do not use your real surname while you are online.

6. Never arrange to meet 'cyber friends' in person without your parents' permission.

7. Never give out your password.

8. Never give out your home address or telephone number.

9. Do not send scanned pictures of yourself unless your parents approve.

10. Leave a website straight away if you find something that is offensive or upsetting. Talk to your parents about it.

Every effort has been made to ensure none of the recommended websites in this book is linked to inappropriate material. However, due to the ever-changing nature of the Internet, the publishers regret they cannot take responsibility for future content of these websites. Therefore, it is strongly advised that children and parents consider the safety guidelines above.

First published in the UK in 2002 by Chrysalis Children's Books PLC
The Chrysalis Building, Bramley Road, London, W10 6SP

Copyright © Chrysalis Children's Books

A ZIGZAG BOOK

All rights reserved. No part of this book may be reproduced or utilized in any form or by any means, electronic or mechanical, including photocopying, recording or by any information storage and retrieval system, without permission in writing from the publisher except by a reviewer who may quote brief passages in a review.

ISBN 1 904516 20 3

British Library Cataloguing in Publication Data for this book is available from the British Library.

Author: Neil Morris
Managing Editor: Nichola Tyrrell
Art Director: Simon Rosenheim
Picture Research: Terry Forshaw
Assistant Editor: Clare Chambers
Assistant Designer: Zeta Jones

Printed and bound in Hong Kong

LONDON BOROUGH OF HILLINGDON LIBRARIES	
01948376 4	
J389	03-Sep-04
PETERS	

CONTENTS

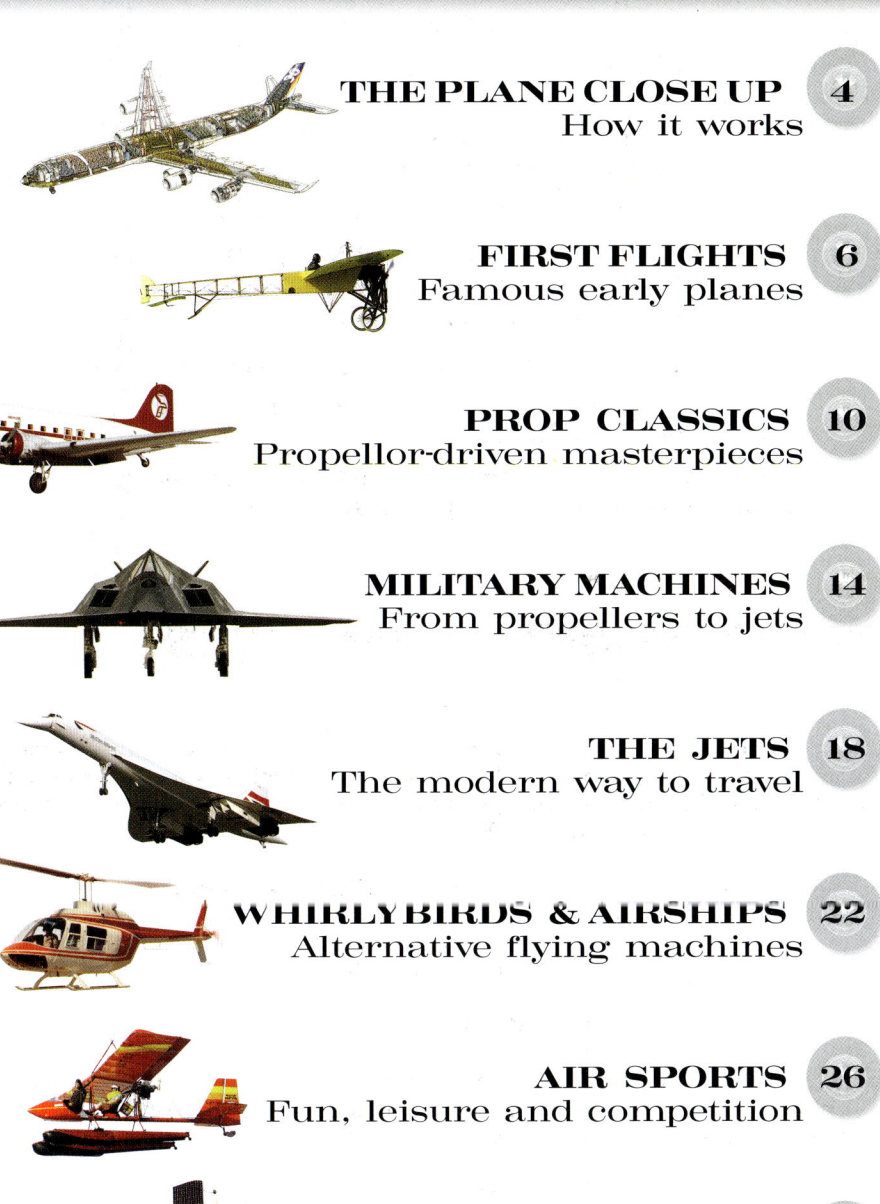

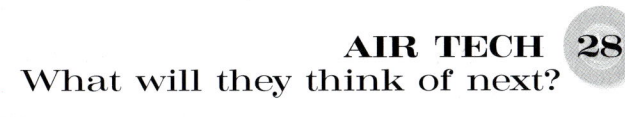

THE PLANE CLOSE UP 4
How it works

FIRST FLIGHTS 6
Famous early planes

PROP CLASSICS 10
Propellor-driven masterpieces

MILITARY MACHINES 14
From propellers to jets

THE JETS 18
The modern way to travel

WHIRLYBIRDS & AIRSHIPS 22
Alternative flying machines

AIR SPORTS 26
Fun, leisure and competition

AIR TECH 28
What will they think of next?

GLOSSARY 30

INDEX 32

THE PLANE CLOSE UP

Many different planes have been designed and built since the first powered aircraft took off a hundred years ago. On the following pages you'll find classic designs, mega powerful jets and discover how the story of aviation developed.

THE COMPONENTS

A small propeller-driven aeroplane may look very different from a powerful modern jetliner but all planes are the same in some ways and are made of similar components. These components – including the engine, wings and control surfaces – are there to help make a plane fly.

This big aeroplane is a passenger airliner. It is powered by four jet engines. Two engines are attached to each wing.

MEGA UPLIFTING
Sir George Cayley (1773-1857) was the first to show how wings with a curved top edge work better. He showed that faster air flowing over the top of a wing has less pressure. This means that slower air beneath the wings has greater pressure and so pushes the plane up into the air.

Nose wheels, part of the undercarriage.

The flight deck, where the captain and first officer sit. A flight engineer sits behind them.

The fuselage, or main body, of a small aircraft is usually a single shell. Larger airliners, like this commercial jet, need braces to add extra strength to the body.

INTERNET LINK
http://www.howstuffworks.com/airplane.htm
Lots of facts and explanations of aerodynamic forces and the way flight works.

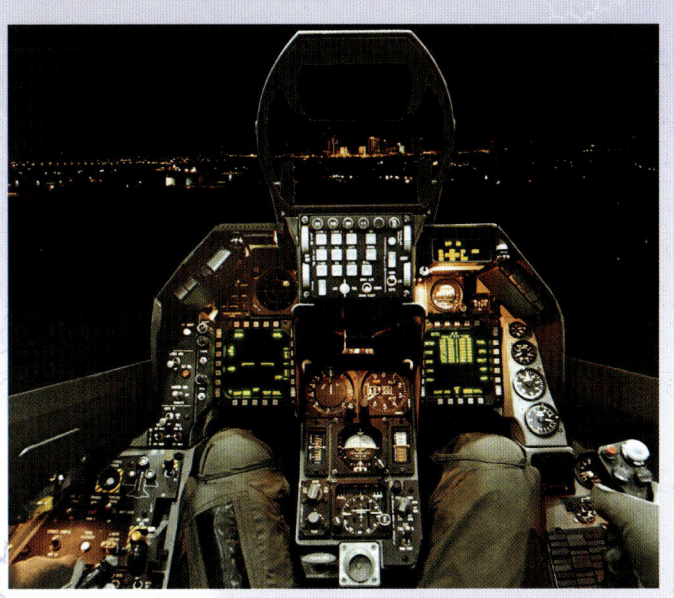

THE FLIGHT DECK

The first planes had a few simple instruments to help the pilot fly. Today, the cockpit is full of dials and screens called CRTs (or cathode ray tubes, like TV monitors). These give pilots all the information they need, including speed, altitude and direction. There are also radar screens and map displays, and lamps light up to warn the pilot of any problems.

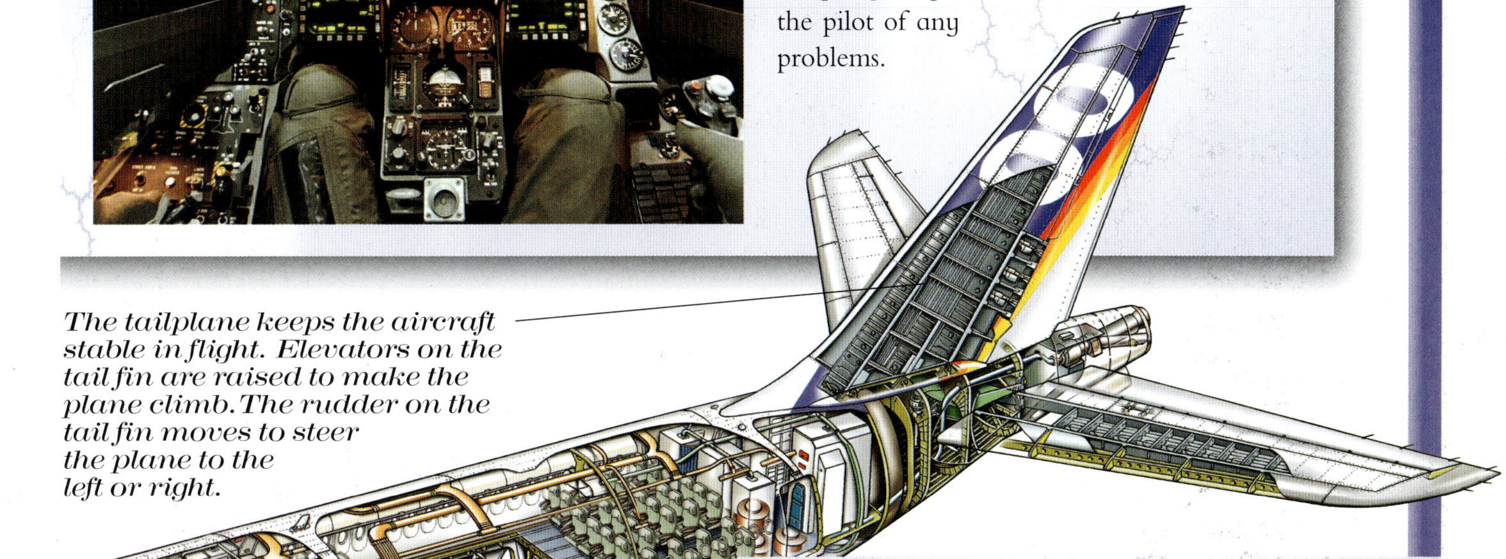

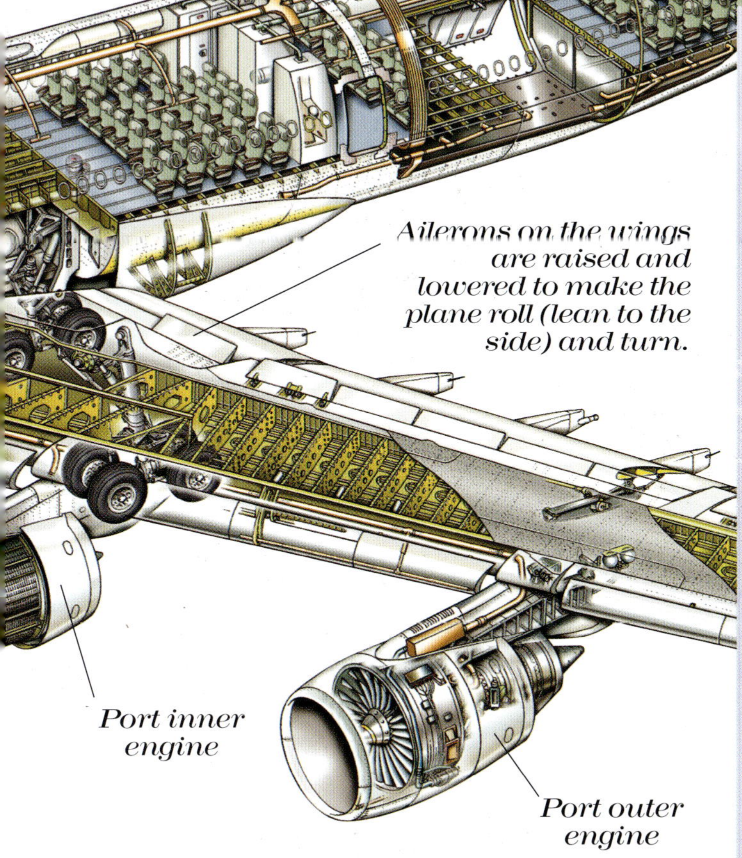

The tailplane keeps the aircraft stable in flight. Elevators on the tail fin are raised to make the plane climb. The rudder on the tail fin moves to steer the plane to the left or right.
Ailerons on the wings are raised and lowered to make the plane roll (lean to the side) and turn.
Port inner engine
Port outer engine

FORCES OF FLIGHT

• Lift pushes a plane up into the air. The wings create enough lift to overcome a plane's weight.

N208LP

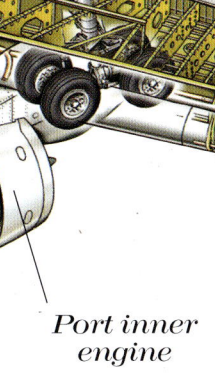

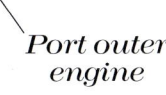

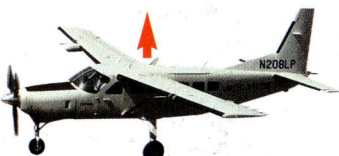

• Thrust pushes a plane through the air. An engine is needed to create enough thrust to overcome a plane's drag (see force no. 4).

N208LP

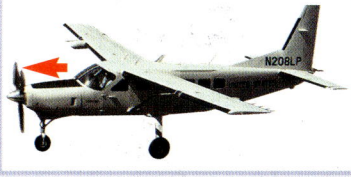

• The plane's weight is a negative force, pulling it down to earth.

N208LP

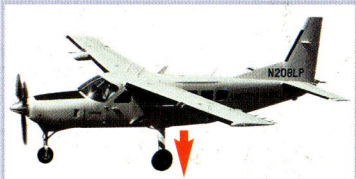

• The negative force of drag is caused by air resistance. It tries to slow a plane down.

N208LP

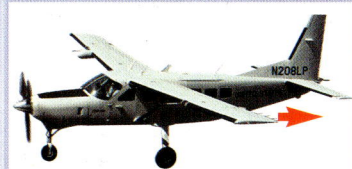

FIRST FLIGHTS

At the very beginning of the 20th century, two American bicycle-makers built their own full-size gliders, as well as a specially designed petrol engine. Then they put all their expertise together to build the world's first successful powered aeroplane, which they called *Flyer*. The two men were brothers – Wilbur and Orville Wright – the pioneers of aviation.

The picture below shows a fine replica of the Wrights' Flyer.

WRIGHT BROTHERS' FLYER

This famous photo shows the moment when Flyer *first took off from its guide rail, with Orville Wright as pilot while Wilbur looks on.*

MEGA WOODEN *Flyer's airframe was made of ash and spruce wood. The wooden wings were covered with linen and stiffened with bracing wires.*

LEONARDO DA VINCI

Four hundred years before the Wright brothers' success, a great Italian painter, sculptor and scientist designed several flying machines. Leonardo da Vinci (1452-1519) bought caged birds in the market and then set them free. He studied the way they flew and drew up his own ideas for human flight. The pilot was supposed to lie down in this machine, called an ornithopter (right). Leonardo's ideas were brilliant for the time, but his flying machines never flew.

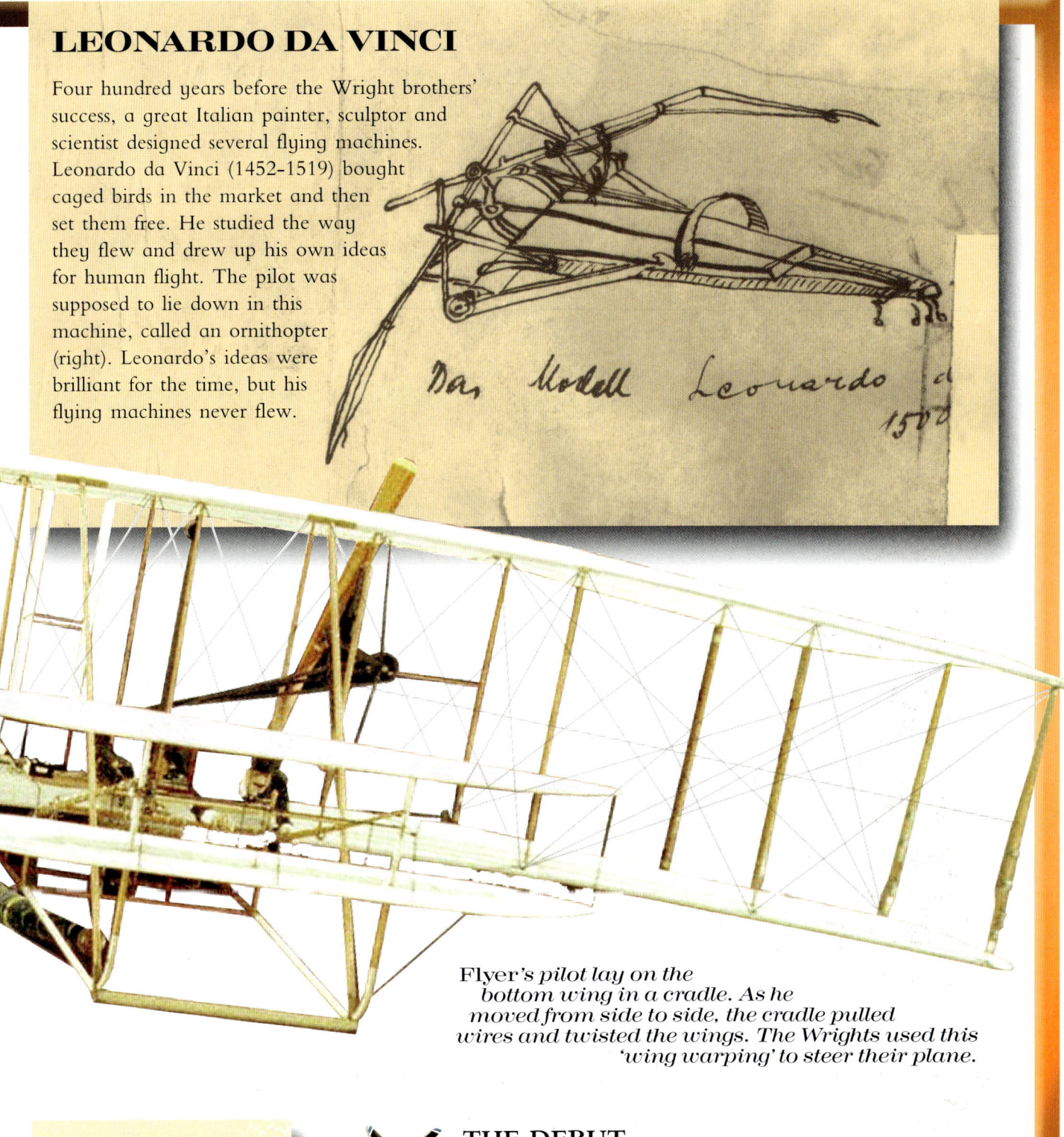

Flyer's pilot lay on the bottom wing in a cradle. As he moved from side to side, the cradle pulled wires and twisted the wings. The Wrights used this 'wing warping' to steer their plane.

MEGA SLIDE
The first aeroplane had no wheels. Its simple undercarriage was made up of bicycle hubs fitted to the front and back. These led the plane along an 18-metre (59-ft) wooden launching rail until it gained enough speed and lift to take off.

THE DEBUT

On 17 December 1903, the Wrights tested their plane on flat land near Kitty Hawk, North Carolina, USA. Eventually, Wilbur piloted the plane and flew for just under a minute. The flight only covered 260 metres (853 ft) but it was the most important event in aviation history.

FIRST FLIGHTS

BLÉRIOT TYPE XI

On 25 July 1909 French aviator Louis Blériot (1872-1936) made the world's first international flight. He took up a newspaper challenge to fly over the English Channel from France to England, and won £1000 (then a great deal of money!) when he made it in his Type XI monoplane. He landed near Dover Castle 36 minutes after taking off from Les Baraques in France. This historic flight made Blériot an overnight celebrity, and more than a hundred of his Type XIs were ordered and built.

MEGA HORSEPOWER
The Type XI's wooden propeller was driven by a motorcycle engine. This produced 25 horsepower — twice as much as the Wrights' Flyer — but it was still only just enough power to get across the Channel.

LILIENTHAL GLIDER

German engineer Otto Lilienthal (1848-96) was another of the great pioneers of aviation. He made more than 2000 flights with his own gliders, which were rather like modern hang-gliders (see page 27). He steered by shifting his weight forwards and backwards, and from side to side. Newspapers called him the 'flying man', but he had to be a tough man too, because he crashed many times. He was eventually killed when his glider crashed on a hillside near Berlin.

MEGA GLIDE
Otto Lilienthal ran along and took off from hilltops. His record glide carried him along for 350 metres (1148 ft).

MEGA LAUNCH
Otto Lilienthal performed most of his gliding from a man-made hill he constructed near his home in Germany.

VICKERS VIMY

The sturdy Vickers Vimy broke all kinds of records, including first across the Atlantic, first from Europe to Australia and first from Britain to South Africa. The journey from England to Australia took 29 days, with many stopovers on the way. This biplane was designed during World War I as a bomber. As soon as the war was over, many were converted to civilian use because they were so strong and reliable. The Vimy was just over 13 metres (43 ft) long with a wingspan of nearly 21 metres (69 ft). Like all early planes, it had an open cockpit for the two-man crew.

INTERNET LINKS
http://www.wrightflyer.org
Learn about testing and flying a replica of the 1903 *Flyer*.
http://www.aviation-history.com
Click on 'Early Years' to find loads of information on the first planes and their pilots.

FIRST ACROSS THE ATLANTIC

In 1918 an English newspaper offered a prize of £10,000 to the first person to fly non-stop across the Atlantic Ocean. On 14 June 1919 two English airmen, Captain John Alcock (1892-1919) and Lieutenant Arthur Whitten Brown (1886-1948), shown right, took off in their Vickers Vimy biplane from the North American coast. Sixteen and a half hours later, pilot Alcock and navigator Brown landed in Ireland, freezing cold and nose-down in a peat bog! Both men were knighted, but tragically Sir John Alcock was killed just six months after his transatlantic flight in a flying accident in France. It was not until 1927 that a solo transatlantic flight was achieved when Charles Lindbergh (1902-74) flew from New York to Paris. His small Ryan monoplane, *Spirit of St. Louis*, achieved an average speed of 173 km/h (107.5 mph).

PROP CLASSICS

In the 1930s aircraft manufacturers started designing planes specially for carrying passengers. The new airlines wanted to attract customers by offering a service that was better than long-distance trains over land or ships across the sea. So they had to make their planes bigger, faster and more comfortable than they were before.

THE DOUGLAS DC-3

The Douglas DC-3 (below) was an early airliner, and it went on to become one of the most successful planes ever built. It first went into service in 1936, and of the 11,000 DC-3s that were made, some are still flying today. The controls on the DC-3 included an automatic pilot and two sets of instruments.

MEGA MILITARY
By 1939, 90 per cent of the USA's air passengers were flying on DC-2s and DC-3s. Their versatility also led to the use of DC-3s in World War II. Known as Skytrains or Skytroopers, they were mass-produced for the military and were used as freight and personnel carriers, ambulances and even glider tugs.

The three-bladed propellers were driven by 1100-horsepower Wright Cyclone engines. Compare that with Blériot's 25 horsepower!

MEGA SNOOZE
The first version of the DC-3 took off as a DST, or Douglas Sleeper Transport. There were 14 sleeping bunks for passengers on overnight flights. Later versions of the plane were called Douglas Dakotas.

The two main undercarriage legs and wheels were raised up into the engine houses after take-off. This helped streamlining and was a new feature in the 1930s.

FLYING IN THE 1930S

This Flying Banana airliner waits for its passengers (38 at most!) at Croydon Airport, south of London. Imperial Airways, which was the first British national airline, was founded in 1924. Croydon was a very advanced airport for its time. In the 1930s many others were still made up of huts and tents. At all airports, passengers had to walk to their plane – there were no jetways or shuttle buses.

DC-3s had a cruise speed of 274 km/h (170 mph).

The DC-3 was almost 20 metres (66 ft) long and had a wingspan of 29 metres (95 ft). It was made from an alloy skin over an alloy frame, joined together by metal rivets.

HOME COMFORTS

In the DC-3, for the first time, up to 28 passengers enjoyed comfortable seats, ventilation and heating. There was a galley for preparing drinks and food, and a toilet. Air travel was certainly improving, and there was even the added service of a stewardess.

PROP CLASSICS

BOEING 247

Boeing was one of the first great aircraft companies. Its founder, William Boeing, learned to fly in 1915 and then started an airmail service between the USA and Canada. In 1933 Boeing introduced his own new aircraft, the 247. This was the world's first streamlined metal airliner, carrying ten passengers and 180 kilograms (396 lb) of mail. It took the 247 20 hours to fly between New York and Los Angeles – 7.5 hours faster than any previous airliners! The 247's two Wasp engines drove adjustable propellers. These allowed the pilot to set the blades at the best angle for a particular speed.

INTERNET LINKS
http://www.aviation-history.com
Discover lots of facts, figures and much more on the history of airliners and other planes.

LOCKHEED CONSTELLATION

The Constellation first took to the air in 1938, but it really developed as a commercial airliner after 1945. It had four prop engines and was one of the first airliners to have a nosewheel instead of a tailwheel, so that the passenger cabin was level with the ground. Lockheed developed more and more different versions of the Constellation, concentrating on comfort. Some had reclining sleeper seats, while others had a luxurious cocktail lounge on board.

MEGA DISTANCE
Lockheed Constellations were used on long-distance routes. In 1946 they were the first planes to fly across the Atlantic from the USA to London's new Heathrow airport.

AMELIA EARHART

In 1932 the American aviator Amelia Earhart became the first woman to fly solo across the Atlantic, in a Lockheed Vega (right). By then she had already helped found an international group of women pilots called the 'Ninety-Nines'. Three years later, she was the first woman to fly solo across the Pacific, from Hawaii to California. Then, in 1937, Earhart tried to fly around the world in a twin-engined Lockheed Electra, with the help of a navigator, Fred Noonan. The plane vanished over the Pacific, but no wreckage has ever been found. The mystery of Amelia Earhart's disappearance has yet to be solved.

HANDLEY PAGE HP42

Do you think the fuselage of the HP42 looks a bit like a banana? Well, that was the nickname of this famous airliner – the Flying Banana. The first Banana (registration code G-AAGX, as shown here) took off in 1940. But although they were very popular with passengers, only eight of these biplanes were ever built. The strange layout of the engines, with two on the upper and two on the lower wing, was supposed to cut down noise inside the passenger cabin. Each upholstered seat had its own heating and ventilation controls – the height of luxury.

MEGA SLOW
The HP42 was designed for comfort, not speed. Flights from England to India took six days, and those to South Africa eight and a half days!

MILITARY MACHINES

Propeller-driven planes played an important part in World War I (1914-18), and aircraft engineers learned a lot about what planes could do. By World War II (1939-45), the invention of the jet engine had changed things dramatically. Jet fighters were much faster, but they were not used in great numbers and so did not have a great effect on the war itself. Nevertheless, the age of the jet was with us.

WWI SOPWITH CAMEL

The Camel was one of the greatest fighter planes of World War I. Flying at up to 185 km/h (115 mph), it was faster than most other fighters, but its powerful 150-horsepower engine made it difficult to fly. The pilot sat in a wicker seat and had to turn the plane to face its target before firing his machine-guns. Like most aircraft of the time, the Camel was a biplane.

MEGA SUCCESS
The Sopwith Camel only entered World War I in 1917, but it was the most successful British fighter. A total of 5490 Camels were built, and they claimed no fewer than 1294 victories over German aircraft.

The Camel's wings and fuselage were made of a wooden frame covered with canvas.

Twin machine-guns on the Sopwith Camel were fired between the propeller blades. The guns fired straight ahead; they could not swivel.

Four 30-millimetre guns fired through slots in the nose of the Me 262.

The Messerschmitt's bubble canopy gave the single pilot good all-round vision.

The Me 262 measured 10.5 metres (34 ft) long and had a wingspan of 12.5 metres (41 ft).

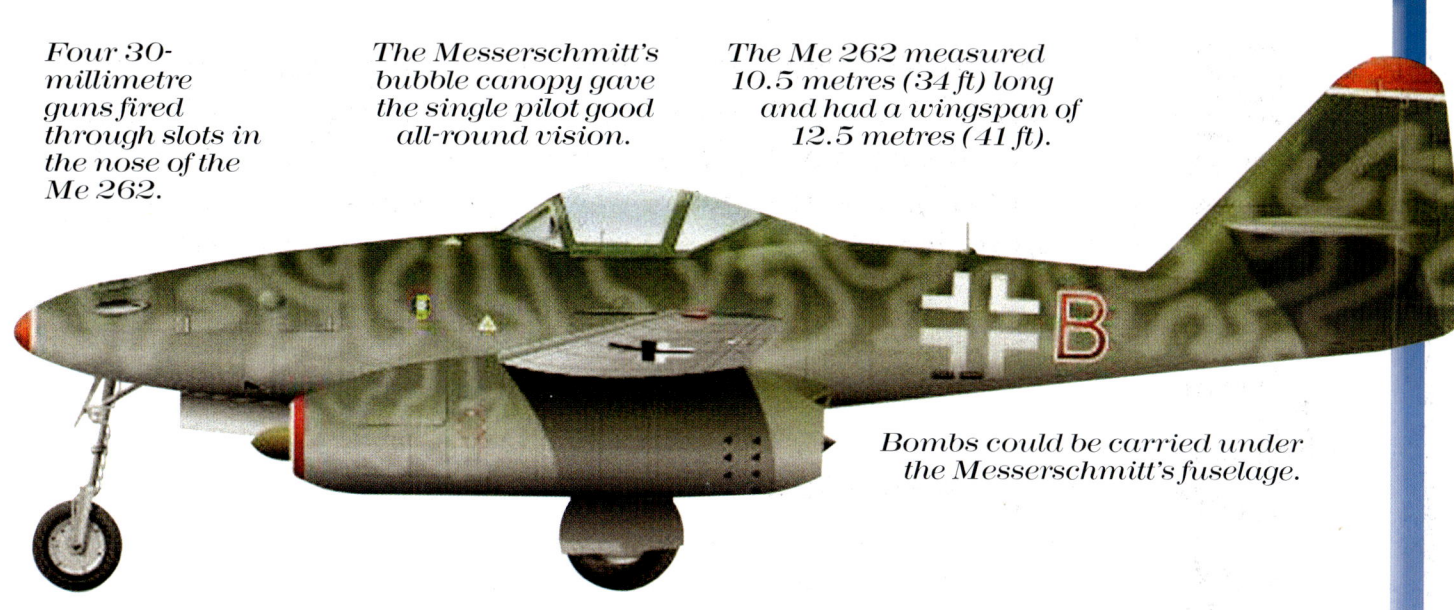

Bombs could be carried under the Messerschmitt's fuselage.

WW2 MESSERSCHMITT ME 262

This famous German fighter plane was designed by Willy Messerschmitt (1898-1978). Powered by two turbojet engines, the plane first flew in 1942. Two years later it became the first jet aircraft in the world to go into full military service. The Me 262 had a top speed of 868 km/h (540 mph) – that's more than four times faster than the Sopwith Camel! It proved to be rather unreliable, however, and many Me 262s crashed.

MEGA QUICK LEARNER
The Camel was designed and built by Sir Thomas Octave Murdoch Sopwith (1888-1989). In 1910 he took up flying, and on 21 November he sat in a biplane for the first time. By tea-time he had qualified for his Pilot's Certificate. The following month, he won a special prize for the longest distance flown in a straight line.

The Camel had a tail skid instead of a rear wheel.

The Sopwith Camel was nearly 6 metres (20 ft) long and had a wingspan of 8.5 metres (28 ft).

FIRST JET ENGINE

English engineer Sir Frank Whittle (1907–96) began work on a jet engine in 1928, while he was a student at the Royal Air Force College in Cranwell. By 1935 he had developed a prototype, and two years later he built and ran the world's first aircraft jet engine. It was fitted to a Gloster Meteor fighter in 1941. By 1944 the RAF were flying squadrons of Meteor jets.

AVRO LANCASTER

The Lancaster was a heavy British bomber used in World War II. It was a four-engined development of the earlier twin-engined Avro Manchester. A modified version of the Lancaster was used in the famous dam-busting raids on northern Germany in 1943. They dropped special bouncing bombs to hit the dams and destroy them. 'Lancs' were also used to lead large groups of bombers on big missions.

MEGA MISSIONS
In 1943 and 1944, a Lancaster plane nicknamed 'The Mother of Them All' flew on 140 missions, more than any other bomber.

SUPERMARINE SPITFIRE

The Spitfire is one of the best-known propeller-driven fighters of all time. It first flew in 1936 and stayed in production right through World War II. By 1945 more than 20,000 Spitfires had been built, and many took part in dogfights during the Battle of Britain. The original Spitfire had a top speed of 571 km/h (355 mph), while the later Spitfire Mark XIX could fly at 718 km/h (446 mph).

INTERNET LINKS
http://www.spitfires.flyer.co.uk
This site is dedicated to the Supermarine Spitfire, with lots of facts on its performance and history.
http://www.rafmuseum.com/index_kids.fm
The kids' site of Britain's Royal Air Force Museum.

MEGA BALANCE
The Harrier jump jet's undercarriage has two outrigger wheels near the end of its wings. These make sure that the aircraft does not tip over. There are also small puffer jets near the wing-tips, controlling the plane when it hovers.

BAe HARRIER JUMP JET

The Harrier fighter bomber first went into service with the Royal Air Force in 1969. It is a 'jump jet' or VTOL (vertical take-off and landing) aircraft, which means it can take off straight upwards, hover and land straight down. To make this possible, the Harrier has special moveable engine nozzles. During normal flight they point backwards, but they can swivel to point downwards and make VTOL possible.

INTERNET LINK
www.fighter-planes.com
Features pictures and information on fighter planes from the 1930s to the present day.

LOCKHEED F-117 NIGHTHAWK

The F-117 Nighthawk bomber is a stealth aircraft. This means that it is specially designed to be very difficult to detect with radar or sonar equipment. The Nighthawk's unusual shape, with many different flat surfaces, helps make this possible by breaking up radar waves. The Lockheed F-117 was first shown in public in 1990. Like all modern military aircraft, many of its features are kept secret. One thing we do know: the Nighthawk is sprayed with special material to absorb radar. The plane is 20 metres (66 ft) long, just 3.8 metres (12.5 ft) high, and has a wingspan of 13 metres (43 ft).

MEGA MIG
The Russian Mikoyan MiG-25 Foxbat is one of the world's fastest combat aircraft. It can fly at more than three times the speed of sound.

17

THE JETS

The first jet planes took to the skies in 1939, and a few were used as fighters during World War II. Jets could fly much faster and higher than propeller-driven planes, and during the 1950s jet airliners – or jetliners – went into service with the world's growing airlines. They made long flights quicker and more comfortable, and before long they could carry more than a hundred passengers each.

MEGA JET
The biggest jetliner of all made its first test flight in 1969. This was the wide-bodied, two-storey Boeing 747, which soon became known as a 'jumbo jet'. Some versions of this huge plane can carry more than 500 passengers.

RUNWAY REQUIREMENTS
Big aircraft need big airports. As larger, heavier jetliners have been introduced, airports have had to lengthen their runways to make sure they have plenty of room for take-off and landing. A 747, for example, needs over 3 kilometres (1.9 mi) of runway to reach its take-off speed.

Winglets curve up at the end of the wings. They help to reduce drag. The Boeing 747-400 has a wingspan of 64.4 metres (211 ft).

MEGA JOURNEY
The 747SP long-range jumbo jet flies the world's longest non-stop route – the 12,050-kilometre (7,483-mi), 15-hour trip from Los Angeles to Sydney.

This jumbo is powered by 4 turbofan jet engines, attached to the wings by pylons. Leading-edge flaps at the front of the wings come out during take-off and landing. These give the plane extra lift at low speeds.

INSIDE A JET ENGINE

Jet engines produce tremendous thrust. The engine sucks in air at the front, and a machine called a compressor raises the air's pressure. This compressed air is then sprayed with aircraft fuel, and the mixture is lit by an electric spark. The burning gases quickly expand and blast out through the back of the engine. As the jets of gas shoot backwards, the aircraft is thrust forwards. There are different kinds of jet engine. Most of today's airliners are powered by turbofans, like the one shown below. This has a large fan at the front, which helps to suck in air. Turbofans are quieter than other jet engines, burning fuel more efficiently and giving more thrust at low speeds.

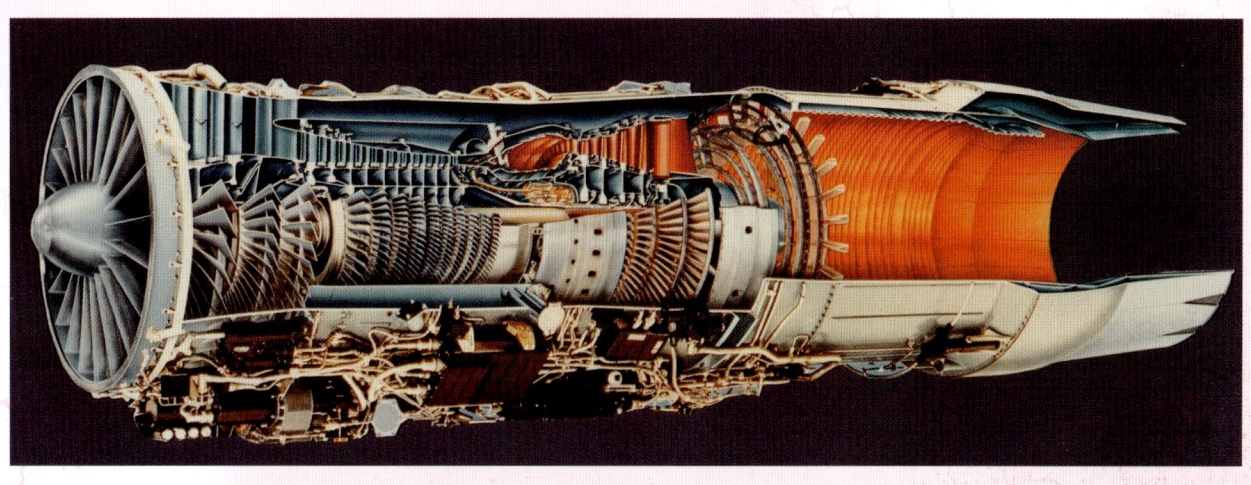

The passengers at the front of the plane are sitting beneath the flight deck, which is on the upper floor.

THE 747's UNDERCARRIAGE

The undercarriage of a Boeing 747 is made up of 18 wheels. There are 4 bogies of 4 wheels under the fuselage and wings, and a two-wheel bogie under the nose. The bogies fold up into the fuselage after take-off. The air in the tyres is kept at very high pressure, to take the huge force when the plane lands.

THE JETS

CONCORDE

Concorde is the world's only supersonic passenger aircraft. It was developed by British and French engineers and went into service with British Airways and Air France in 1976. Travelling faster than the speed of sound means that Concorde can fly from New York to London in less than three hours. Only 16 Concordes have ever been built, however, and after a crash in 2000 they were grounded while safety tests were carried out. In November 2001, with renewed safety features, Concorde took to the skies once again.

MEGA NOSY
In supersonic flight, Concorde's nose points straight ahead. But the pointed nose was designed to droop, so it can be lowered at slower speeds. For take-off and landing, the 'droop snoot' is put right down so that pilots have a clear view ahead.

DE HAVILLAND COMET

The world's first jetliner, the Comet, started flying regularly in 1952. Its first scheduled flight was from London to Johannesburg, South Africa, with five stops on the way. The Comet took 12 hours off the previous flying time on this route. But between 1952 and 1954 Comets were involved in a series of crashes. Tests showed that the fuselage suffered from a problem known as metal fatigue. After four years of improvement, a new, safer Comet took to the air. The aircraft was powered by four de Havilland Ghost turbojet engines which were built into the wings to make the aircraft as streamlined as possible.

LEARJET

Executive aircraft are small jetliners for business people, sports stars and others who can afford to fly them privately. They are sometimes called 'bizjets' (or business jets). This Learjet is just a quarter of the length of a Boeing 747. It has room for two pilots and nine passengers. Some wealthy owners have the cabin of their executive jet specially designed to suit their needs, with armchairs, desks or computer workstations.

> **MEGA SMALL**
> One of the smallest bizjets, the Cessna 525 Citationjet, is just 12 metres (42 ft) long. It has room for two pilots and six passengers.

BOEING 747

The first test flight of a Boeing 747 was made in 1969 near Seattle, USA, where it was built. The giant jumbo made its first passenger flight a year later, flying in the colours of Pan American Airways from New York to London. Over the next seven years, 747s carried more than 134 million passengers all over the world. This Boeing 747 can fly for 14,630 kilometres (9130 mi) without needing to refuel. It cruises at a speed of 980 km/h (612 mph).

> **MEGA SIZE**
> The Boeing 747-400 is 70 metres (231 ft) long, which makes it more than 10 times longer than the Wrights' Flyer. The jumbo's huge baggage hold, beneath the two passenger cabins, holds up to 3400 pieces of luggage. These can be loaded or unloaded in just seven minutes.

INTERNET LINKS
http://www.concordesst.com
A fascinating site with cutaway views.

WHIRLYBIRDS & AIRSHIPS

When people first dreamed of flying, they probably thought of machines like today's helicopters. The great thing about helicopters is that they can fly in any direction – forwards, backwards, sideways or straight up. They can even hover in one place.

VERSATILE 'COPTERS

The first practical helicopters were developed in the late 1930s, and since then they have become an essential part of the flying world. Landing spaces called helipads have been built on top of many skyscrapers, lighthouses and oil-rigs. Small whirlybirds are very manoeuvrable, while giant choppers are strong lifters and are widely used in industry and as military aircraft.

The pilot uses a collective stick to make the helicopter go up or down, and a cyclic stick to change direction. Both sticks work by changing the pitch, or angle, of the rotor blades.

MEGA LIFT
The Boeing Vertol Chinook twin-rotor chopper is big and strong. This heavy-lift model can carry up to 55 passengers and lift huge weights such as army tanks.

HELICOPTER RESCUE

Helicopters can land almost anywhere, but their greatest advantage to the world's rescue services is that they can hover in one place. This means they can be used for the most dramatic rescues, such as lifting sailors from sinking ships, saving climbers trapped on cliffs and mountains, or rescuing people cut off by floods, fires and other natural disasters. Lines can be lowered from the aircraft to hoist up victims in harnesses. Helicopters are also used by the emergency services as air ambulances.

The two rotor blades of the Bell Jetranger (below) are driven by the engine. They whirl round like a propeller and give both lift and thrust.

While hovering, helicopters can spin so the pilot can look in any direction.

The tail fin at the end of the boom acts as a stabilizer and a rudder. The small tail-rotor stops the helicopter turning round in the opposite direction to the spin of the main rotor blades. It also acts as a rudder.

The landing skids are sometimes replaced by wheels or floats.

THE FIRST CHOPPERS

The first helicopter to fly successfully never went beyond the prototype stage. It was built in 1936 by Frenchman Louis Breguet and had two rotors, with an open framework fuselage. This hélicoptère flew for over an hour. Three years later, the Russian-born American Igor Sikorsky invented a better, single-rotor machine, which included a tail-rotor. By 1944 the Sikorsky R-4B was in full production in the USA.

MEGA WHIRL
In 1996 Ron Bower and John Williams of the USA took off from London in a Bell helicopter. They returned 17 days later, having whirled all the way around the world.

WHIRLYBIRDS & AIRSHIPS

SKYSHIP

Modern airships are filled with helium gas, which is safe because it cannot burn or explode. They do not have a rigid structure, but keep their shape because of gas pressure. They are popular for advertising, aerial filming and special events. The Skyship 600 normally cruises at 55 km/h (34 mph) at a height of 6000 metres (19,700 ft). Its two propellers are driven by Porsche engines, and it can stay in the air for up to 50 hours without refuelling.

MEGA DIRIGIBLE
The Skyship is a dirigible airship, which means that it can be steered. The four control surfaces near the back can be moved by the pilot. The propellers are in swivelling ducts, which turn to help with take-off and landing.

MEGA FACT
The Skyship 600 carries up to 13 passengers. The overall length of the airship is 59 metres (193.5 ft).

HINDENBURG

The German *Hindenburg* was the largest airship ever built. It had an aluminium alloy frame and was a giant 245 metres (804 ft) long. The gondola carried up to 70 passengers, and the four diesel engines gave it an incredible top speed of 140 km/h (87 mph). The *Hindenburg* first flew in 1936 and began regular transatlantic flights. It had one big problem, however. This airship was filled with hydrogen gas, which burns very easily. On 3 May 1937, the airship burst into flames near its landing dock in New Jersey. The *Hindenburg* burned out in 32 seconds, killing 36 people. It was not the only hydrogen-airship disaster, and the great airship age of the 1930s soon ended.

MEGA FAST
On its round-the-world journey, the Breitling Orbiter reached altitudes of 11,000 metres (36,000 ft) and speeds of 176 km/h (105 mph).

BREITLING ORBITER

The Breitling Orbiter 3 is an enormous mixed balloon. This means that it has a cell of helium gas inside a large envelope of hot air. Helium is lighter than air, and hot air rises, so the combination is very effective. The air is heated by gas burners. In March 1999, Brian Jones of Britain and Bertrand Piccard of Switzerland became the first humans to fly nonstop around the world in a balloon. Their Orbiter flew for just over 19 days and covered almost 43,000 kilometres (26,724 mi). It measures 55 metres (180 ft) in height with a total weight of 8 tonnes (that's heavier than a Learjet!). The Orbiter's enclosed capsule contains a bunk for one of the two pilots to sleep in, a water-heater and a toilet.

INTERNET LINK
http://www.helicopters.com
Get the latest whirlybird news.

In an emergency, such as landing in strong winds or in the sea, the balloon can be released from the gondola capsule.

FULL OF HOT AIR
The hot air for hot-air balloons is made by burning liquid propane gas. Pilots control their height by heating or cooling the air in the balloon. But they cannot control direction, except by looking for air currents blowing in particular directions. Ballooning has become a very popular sport and balloons now come in more and more bizarre shapes, like this motorcycle (left)!

AIR SPORTS

There are all sorts of air sports, involving many different kinds of flying machines. Most are done just for the fun of it, but there are also competitions, based mainly on style, speed or distance covered. Some of the craft have engines, but others simply glide along on the breeze.

MEGA PAPER PLANE
In 1970 a full-size glider was built at Ohio State University, USA, using only paper, glue and masking tape. The paper plane and its pilot were towed into the air by a car and flew at a speed of 96 km/h (60 mph).

MODERN GLIDER

The most difficult part of flying a glider – a plane with no engine – is getting airborne in the first place. The glider is either pulled along on a long cable by a car or a winch on the ground, or it is given a tow into the air by a small powered plane. Once aloft, pilots try to get a lift on warm currents of air called thermals.

MICROLIGHT

Microlight and ultralight aircraft are the smallest powered planes. They carry up to two people, and many are assembled from a kit before use. This model (left) has a fixed wing, while other, smaller microlights have a flexible wing like a hang-glider. Some have wheels, while this model takes off and lands on water.

WING WALKING

Wing walkers really know what it is like to fly like a bird! They bravely stand on the wing while an aircraft is in flight, attached by a lifeline in case they lose their balance. The world record for the longest wing walk stands at more than three hours.

AEROBATICS

In the sport of aerobatics, pilots in single-engined light aircraft are judged on special moves such as loops, spins and rolls. At air shows and other events, display aerobatics by jet aircraft are popular with spectators. The Red Arrows (left) are a world-famous display team who never fail to thrill with their amazing formation flying.

HANG-GLIDER

Hang-glider pilots lie in a harness beneath a large kite-shaped wing, or sail. They hold on to a control bar, and use this to shift their weight and steer the craft, following thermals when they can. To take off, pilots run into the wind on a hill or cliff-top. Competitions are judged on distance and speed, but most hang-gliding is done just for the experience of flying like a bird.

INTERNET LINKS
http://www.actionairsports.com
Information on aviation sport including ballooning, skydiving, hang-gliding and more.
http://www.deltaweb.co.uk/reds
Official home of the Red Arrow team.

AIR TECH

Today's inventors and engineers make sure that aviation keeps changing. Modern developments include greater use of computer technology and new sources of flight power such as solar energy. Aircraft and airports get bigger and more efficient, in attempts to make flying more comfortable. We can only imagine how things will change in the next century of powered flight.

MEGA AIRSPEED
The world airspeed record is held by a Lockheed SR-71A Blackbird jet, which flew at an incredible 3,529 km/h (2192 mph).

BELUGA AIRBUS

The Airbus Super Transporter A300-600ST Beluga not only has one of the longest aircraft names, it is also the world's most spacious airliner. Its huge, bulbous cargo compartment is most useful for carrying other aircraft parts. The Beluga (named after the white whale of the Arctic) can carry a load of over 45 tonnes.

KANSAI AIRPORT

This supermodern airport stands on a man-made island in Osaka Bay, Japan. The island, which took five years to build in the shallow bay, is 4.5 kilometres (2.8 mi) long and 1.25 kilometres (0.8 mi) wide. It is connected to the mainland by a long, two-level bridge, with railway lines on the lower level and a road on top. High-speed boats also reach the airport from the port of Kobe in 30 minutes. The airport's terminal, made of curved steel and glass, is designed in the shape of an aircraft wing.

28

HELIOS SOLAR WING

Helios (named after the Greek god of the sun) is a solar-powered 'flying wing' aircraft being developed by NASA in the USA. It is flown by remote control by a pilot on the ground, and powered by 14 propellers driven by electric motors. The motors can be powered by batteries, but will eventually be driven by solar energy collected from the top side of the wing. With a wingspan of 75 metres (247 ft), Helios has a length of just 4 metres (12 ft)!

MEGA FLIGHT

The aim of the Helios project is for the plane to fly for at least four days non-stop at a speed of up to 40 km/h (25 mph). Once the solar technology is ready, it should be able to fly continuously for up to six months at a time! During the night, the engines will use energy stored during daylight.

HMDS

Modern helmets for fighter pilots have displays projected on to them. This means that the pilot can look outside the cockpit, rather than down at aircraft instruments, while information is shown inside the visor. The system is called HMDS – Helmet-mounted Display and Sight. It can also be used to measure the pilot's line of sight, so that he can aim weapons by looking at the target. Other similar systems are used to display information on the cockpit shield in front of the pilot.

MEGA EJECTION

Ejector seats use rockets to blast a pilot out of the cockpit in an emergency. The latest seats can save a pilot even if the plane is about to crash or is very near the ground.

INTERNET LINK

http://www.pbs.org/wgbh/nova/supersonic
Explore the future of air travel with diagrams, animation and text.
http://www.dfrc.nasa.gov
This is the site of the Flight Research Centre where you can check out the latest prototypes.

GLOSSARY

AILERON A hinged flap on an aeroplane's wing that turns up or down to make the plane bank and turn.

AIRFRAME The whole structure of an aircraft, excluding the engines.

AIRLINER A large passenger aircraft.

BIPLANE An aeroplane with two sets of wings, one above the other.

BOGIE A group of wheels forming part of the undercarriage.

CHOPPER A slang name for a helicopter.

COCKPIT The cabin at the front of an aircraft where the pilot and crew sit.

CRT Cathode ray tubes; visual display moniters used by pilots.

MEGA WINGS
A biplane has two sets of wings, a triplane has three ... and in 1904 Horatio Philips built a plane with 20 sets of wings! Unfortunately his so-called multiplane failed to take off.

DIRIGIBLE An airship that can be steered.

DOGFIGHT Close combat between fighter planes.

DRAG The force caused by the resistance of air that has to be overcome for a plane to fly.

ELEVATOR A hinged flap at the tail of a plane that turns up or down to make the plane go up or down.

FUSELAGE The main body of an aircraft.

GLIDER A plane that flies without the use of an engine.

MEGA SPEED
Aviators talk about airspeed and ground speed. A plane's airspeed is relative to the air through which it flies. Its ground speed is relative to the ground over which it is flying.

HELIPAD A landing and take-off area for helicopters, often on the roof of a building.

HORSEPOWER A unit used to measure the power of engines (which used to be compared to the power of a number of horses).

LIFT The force that pushes a plane up into the air.

MONOPLANE An aeroplane with a single set of wings.

NAVIGATOR A person who plans and directs the flight path of an aircraft.

PROPELLER A set of turning blades driven by an engine that push a plane through the air.

RUDDER A hinged flap at the tail of a plane that can turn to change the direction in which a plane flies.

STREAMLINED Designed with a shape that slips easily through the air.

SUPERSONIC Flying faster than the speed of sound.

TAILPLANE Fin, rudder and elevators of an aircraft.

THRUST The force that pushes an aeroplane through the air.

TURBOFAN A jet engine with a large fan at the front.

UNDERCARRIAGE The wheels or other structures beneath an aircraft that support it on the ground.

WINGSPAN The distance between the wing tips of an aircraft.

MEGA BIRD
The word 'aviation', which means the flying of aircraft, comes from the Latin word for 'bird'. From the earliest times, people have wanted to fly like birds.

INDEX

A
aerobatics 27
air sports 26-27
airport, Kansai 28
airships 24
Alcock, John 9
Atlantic crossings 9
Avro,
    Lancaster 16
    Manchester 16

B
BAe Harrier,
    Jump Jet 17
Battle of Britain 16
Bell,
    Jetranger 22-23
Beluga airbus 28
Blériot,
    Louis 8
    Type XI 8
Boeing,
    247 12
    747 18-19, 21
    Vertol Chinook 22
    William 12
Bower, Ron 23
Breguet, Louis 23
Breitling Orbiter 25
Brown, Arthur
    Whitten 9

C
Cayley, George 4
Cessna 21
Concorde 20
CRTs 5

D
Da Vinci, Leonardo 7
De Havilland,
    Comet 20
    Ghost 20
Douglas
    Dakota 10
    DC-3 10-11
    Sleeper Transport 10

E
Earhart, Amelia 13

F
fighter planes 14-17
flight deck 5
Flyer 6-7, 21
Flying Banana 11, 13
forces of flight 5

G
glider 26

H
Handley Page,
    HP42 13
hang-glider 27
helicopters 22-23
Helios Solar Wing 29
Hindenburg 24
HMDS helmets 29
hot-air balloons 25

I
internet links 4, 9, 12, 16, 17, 21, 25, 27, 29,

J
jet engine 19
jets 4-5, 18-21
Jones, Brian 25
jumbo jet 18

K
Kansai airport 28

L
Learjet 21, 25
Lilienthal,
    glider 8
    Otto 8
Lindbergh, Charles 9
Lockheed,
    Constellation 12
    F-117
    Nighthawk 17
    SR-71A
    Blackbird 28
    Vega 13

M
Messerschmidt,
    ME 262 15
    Willy 15
microlight 26
Mikoyan MiG 17
Murdoch, Thomas Octave 15

P
Philips, Horatio 30
Piccard, Bertrand 25

R
Royal Air Force 17

S
Sikorsky,
    Igor 23
    R-4B 23
Skyship 600 24
Sopwith,
    Camel 14, 15
Spirit of St. Louis 9
Spitfire 16,
    Mark XIX 16

V
Vickers Vimy 9
VTOL 17

W
Whittle, Sir Frank 15
Williams, John 23
wing walking 27
World War I 9, 14
World War II 14, 15, 16, 18
Wright,
    Orville and Wilbur 6-7

Picture Credits

Front Cover: E. de Malglaiva/The Flight Collection

4/5 John Marsden-Tim Hall/The Flight Collection; 6/7 AFP Photos; 7 Hulton|Archive; 8T AFP Photos; 8B Hulton|Archive; 11 Hulton|Archive; 12T George Hall/Corbis; 12B John H. Clark/Corbis; 13T Hulton|Archive; 14 Skyscan/R. Winslade; 16T Richard Napper; 16B Richard Napper; 20T Trent Jones/The Flight Collection; 20B Tony Hobbs/The Flight Collection; 23 Digital Vision; 24B Hulton-Deutsch Collection/Corbis; 25T AFP Photos; 25B Bettmann/Corbis; 26T Joseph Sohm-Chromo Sohm Inc./Corbis; 26B Eye Ubiquitous/Corbis; 27T Vince Streano/Corbis; 27C Gunter Marx Photography/Corbis; 27B Morton Beebe, S.F./Corbis; 28T AFP Photos; 28B Kansai Airport; 29T AFP Photos; 30/31 Art-Tech

All other pictures Chrysalis Images